SEASONAL WEATHER

AUTUMN
WEATHER

John Mason

Seasonal Weather

Spring Weather
Summer Weather
Autumn Weather
Winter Weather

Cover: Early morning in autumn in Vermont, USA.

Opposite: Bare trees and morning mist shortly after dawn in late autumn.

C603928699

Cố
/
J551.5

Edited by Sarah Doughty
Series designed by Derek Lee

First published in 1990 by
Wayland (Publishers) Ltd
61, Western Road, Hove
East Sussex, BN3 1JD, England

© Copyright 1990 Wayland (Publishers) Ltd

British Library Cataloguing in Publication Data
Mason, John
    Autumn weather. – (seasonal weather)
    1. Weather
    1. Title II. Series
    551.5

    ISBN 1–85210–920–3

Typeset by Nicola Taylor, Wayland
Printed and bound by Casterman S.A., Belgium

CONTENTS

The seasons

In some parts of the world the weather changes at different times of the year. These changes in the weather are called seasons. There are four seasons – spring, summer, autumn and winter. Each season is marked by differences in the length of day and night, and each one has a particular type of weather. It takes many weeks for one season to change to the next.

In the **tropics**, the weather varies little from one season to another. Day and night are of roughly equal length all year and it is always warm. Near the **poles** it is always bitterly cold. They have only two real seasons, summer and winter, but the **Arctic** does have a very short spring and autumn.

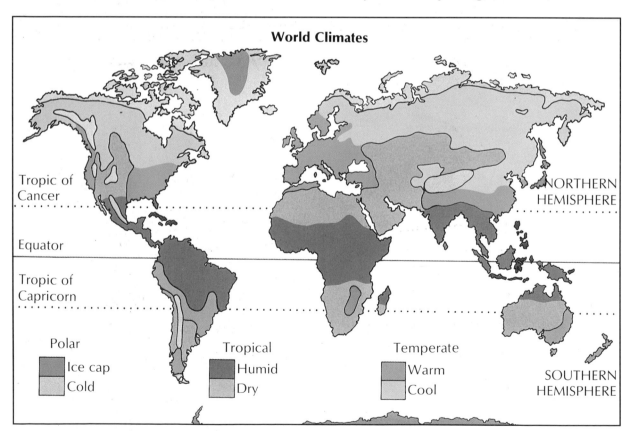

World Climates

Tropic of Cancer

Equator

Tropic of Capricorn

NORTHERN HEMISPHERE

SOUTHERN HEMISPHERE

Polar
Ice cap
Cold

Tropical
Humid
Dry

Temperate
Warm
Cool

Autumn is one of four seasons that occur in temperate regions.

The beautiful autumn colours of the forests near Inuvik, Canada which lies just inside the Arctic Circle.

It is only the **temperate regions** between the poles and the tropics which have clear seasonal changes, without the extremes of heat or cold.

The autumn months mark the transition between summer and winter. The long, warm days gradually give way to short, cooler days. As the hours of daylight grow shorter and the nights grow longer and colder, we feel the approach of winter.

A typical scene in woodlands of temperate regions in autumn.

Why seasons occur

As the Earth moves around the Sun, it spins like a top on its axis. This axis is not upright, but leans over at an angle of 23.5°. It is this tilt which causes the seasons. As the Earth goes round the Sun, this tilt means that first one **hemisphere**, then the other leans towards the Sun.

Between 21 March and 23 September, the northern hemisphere is tilted towards the Sun. The Sun is then higher in the sky at midday and spends longer above the **horizon**. This makes the days long and the nights short, and the weather is warm. At the same time in the southern hemisphere, the Sun is much lower in the sky and the ground receives less warmth. Here the days are short and the nights long and it is cooler.

Between 23 September and 21 March this situation is reversed, and it is colder in the northern hemisphere and warmer in the south.

In the northern hemisphere, autumn begins about 23 September. This is one of the dates when day and night are of equal length all over the

Mist gathers in the Aire Valley in Yorkshire, Britain during autumn evenings. Autumn evenings draw in earlier as winter approaches.

world. It is called an equinox. In the southern hemisphere, the seasons are reversed and this equinox is the beginning of spring. The southern autumn begins about 21 March, the equinox which also marks the beginning of northern spring.

Northern Hemisphere			
Autumn	Winter	Spring	Summer
September	December	March	June
October	January	April	July
November	February	May	August
Spring	Summer	Autumn	Winter
Southern Hemisphere			

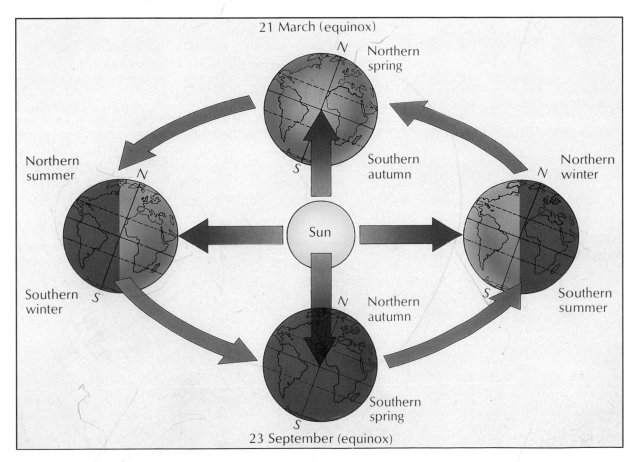

As the Earth orbits the Sun, the tilt of its axis affects the amount of sunlight and heat that reaches different parts of the Earth through the year. This causes the changing seasons.

The autumn season

Autumn weather is very changeable. Some days are warm and sunny, but it can get very cold at night. Autumn is warmer than spring because the land, air and sea retain some of the heat of the summer sunshine and take time to cool.

In autumn many things around us begin to look different. As the weather turns colder, the leaves of deciduous trees change colour, die and fall to the ground. The leaves turn brown, gold and red, and brilliant autumn colours can be seen in gardens and orchards everywhere. They are a beautiful sight in the woodlands and forests in the northern and southern temperate regions.

Autumn is also a season of storms in many places, especially in the western Atlantic, Pacific and Indian Oceans. These storms form in the steamy heat of the tropics

In Japan, the leaves of the trees turn brilliant colours in autumn.

at the end of summer, and move into the temperate regions. As these storms move across the warm ocean waters they may develop into tropical cyclones. These are violent storms that can cause great destruction.

The first heavy frosts of the approaching winter season usually appear in autumn, and fog is also common. The frosts mark the end of the growing season for many plants and crops.

▲ **Thick frost covers this field of cabbages following a freezing cold autumn night.**

Harvesting wheat takes place in early autumn in the USA.

The Earth's winds

Autumn is often a season of strong winds and storms. Wind is simply fast-moving air that results from differences in air pressure. Warm air always rises, creating an area of low pressure. Cooler air moves in to replace it, and as it is heavier it sinks, creating an area of high pressure.

Near the **Equator** the air is always warm, and as it rises it presses down less heavily on the ground. This area of low pressure is called the Equatorial Trough. The Equatorial Trough moves seasonally north and south of the Equator. It is furthest north in August and furthest south in February. Storms often occur in this area in the early autumn and move towards the temperate regions.

The warm air rising at the Equator spreads out towards the north and south. In the 'horse latitudes' at 30° north and 30° south, this air cools and sinks again forming bands of high pressure. This is an area covered by deserts and has almost no rain.

At the poles the air is always cold. It sinks to the ground and high pressure areas develop. The cool polar air spreads out towards the

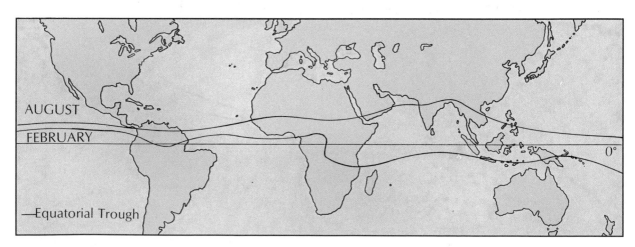

The Equatorial Trough is an area of low pressure. This diagram shows the position of the Equatorial Trough in February and August.

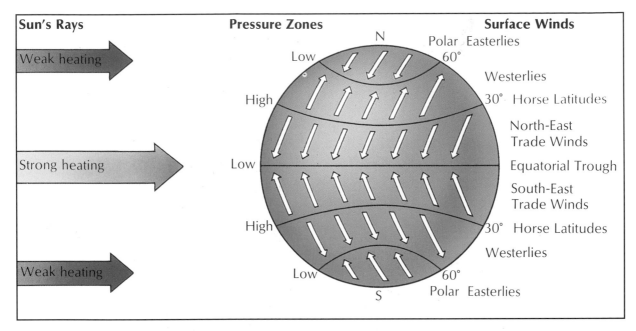

Sun's Rays	Pressure Zones	Surface Winds

Sun's Rays

Weak heating

Strong heating

Weak heating

Pressure Zones

N

Low

High

Low

High

Low

S

Surface Winds

Polar Easterlies
60°

Westerlies
30° Horse Latitudes

North-East
Trade Winds

Equatorial Trough

South-East
Trade Winds

30° Horse Latitudes

Westerlies

60°
Polar Easterlies

The Sun heats the Earth unevenly creating differences in air temperature. High or low pressure areas develop when warm air rises and cool air sinks. Air moving from high to low pressure causes the winds.

Equator. It rises again at 60° north and 60° south in the temperate regions, and creates bands of low pressure. Air at high pressure will always try to move into a neighbouring area of low pressure and this continual motion causes the winds to blow.

In both hemispheres, strong winds called the **Trade Winds** blow towards the Equator and converge in the Equatorial Trough.

Flying a kite on a windy day.

Autumn fog and frosts

As the Sun's rays warm the seas, lakes and rivers, some water **evaporates** and is absorbed by the air above. It is held as an invisible gas called **water vapour**. Air can only hold a certain amount of water vapour at a particular

Warm moist air near valley slopes cools, becomes heavier and slides downwards into the valley. Cooling causes water vapour in the air to condense into fog.

temperature. Warm air can hold more water vapour than cold air. When air cannot absorb any more water vapour it is said to be saturated. If saturated air then cools below a certain temperature (called its **dewpoint**), some of the water vapour **condenses** out into tiny water droplets.

On clear, cold autumn nights, the ground cools

A layer of white frost coats the tips of leaves in autumn.

quickly because there are no clouds to hold in the heat. As the warm, moist air near the ground cools to below the dewpoint, its water vapour condenses into millions of tiny droplets. This is fog or mist.

If the dewpoint is below freezing point (0°C, 32°F), water vapour will condense out of saturated air not as a liquid but as white, needle-shaped crystals of ice. This is hoar frost. It forms first as a white layer on the ground where cold air has settled. The first heavy frosts usually occur on calm, cloudless nights.

The Sun's warmth should soon clear early morning autumn mists.

13

The formation of clouds

When warm, moist air rises into the upper atmosphere where it is colder it becomes saturated. Clouds form when this saturated air is cooled below its dewpoint. Some of the water vapour in the air condenses into tiny water droplets, which collect together to become visible as clouds.

If a cloud enters a colder region, more water vapour condenses into droplets and the cloud grows. If it is cooled still further, the water droplets collide with each other and become larger and heavier until they fall as rain.

Clouds are formed in several ways. Convection cloud is formed when warm air rises from hot land or ocean water and is cooled below its dewpoint temperature.

Clouds form over hills and mountains when warm, moist air is forced up over high ground and its water vapour condenses. This is called orographic cloud.

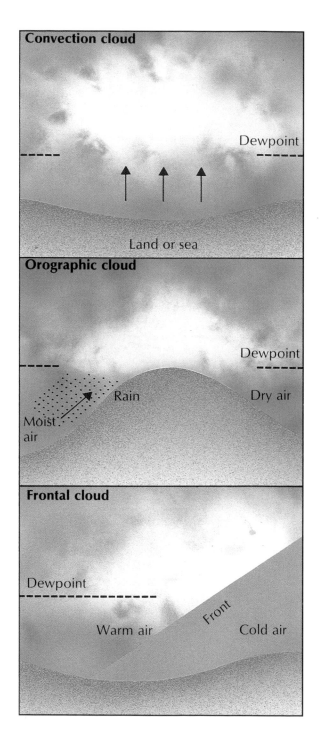

The formation of convection, orographic and frontal clouds.

Clouds also form at cold or warm **fronts**. A cold front occurs when advancing cold air meets stationary warm air. The warm air rises above the cold air and cools, forming clouds. A warm front occurs when moving warm air meets stationary cold air. Again, warm air rises and cools and cloud is formed.

Greatest Rainfall

The wettest place on Earth lies in the Equatorial Trough.

In the dense rainforest of Mt Wai-ale-ale in the Hawaiian Islands, rain usually falls 335 days per year and sometimes 350 days per year.

Clouds race over ripe fields of wheat in autumn and may bring rain showers shortly.

Blue skies and red sunsets

Sunlight, or white light, is made up of the seven different colours of the **spectrum**. They are red, orange, yellow, green, blue, indigo and violet. Each colour of light travels as a wave and has a different **wavelength**.

As sunlight passes through the atmosphere, it is scattered in all directions by tiny dust particles or water droplets. Different wavelengths of light are scattered by different amounts. Blue light is scattered more than any other

A clear, deep blue sky on a fine autumn day in Illinois, USA.

colour. As the air contains millions of tiny particles and droplets, the scattered light is easily seen. This is why the sky looks blue. If it were not for this effect, a clear sky would look black except near the Sun.

At sunset or sunrise, the Sun's rays have to pass through a greater thickness of

A triangular glass prism disperses white light into the colours of the spectrum.

The Sun glows fiery red in colour as it sinks low in the sky.

air than when the Sun is high in the sky. Most of the light at the blue end of the spectrum is scattered out by tiny particles in this thick layer and cannot be seen. So, far more red light than blue light reaches your eyes, and the Sun appears deep orange-red in colour. Any clouds near the Sun also look pink because they reflect the light of the Sun.

During autumn, the Sun is lower in the sky than in summer. The Sun sets earlier each evening as winter draws near.

Hurricanes, cyclones and typhoons

The most destructive autumn storms are tropical cyclones. These storms are called hurricanes in the Atlantic Ocean, typhoons in the Pacific, cyclones in the Indian Ocean and willy-willies in Australia. The most common types of storms are those which form over the warm waters either side of the Equatorial Trough where the sea surface temperatures are above 27°C (80.6°F). Water vapour rises to form towering clouds, pushing huge amounts of heat into the atmosphere. This mixture of heat and water vapour is the fuel that powers these violent storms.

Hurricanes may begin as a group of thunderstorms in west Africa. Huge circulating funnels of low pressure air then move westwards over the warm ocean waters, drawing up huge quantities of water vapour. They may grow into a cluster of severe thunderstorms or even a hurricane.

Strong winds have caused a tree to fall on a car during the October 1987 storm in Britain.

The Great Storm

One of the worst storms to hit the British Isles occurred on the night of 15–16 October 1987.

Gusts of wind of speeds of up to 170 kph were recorded, causing great damage and 15 million trees to fall. Only eighteen people lost their lives.

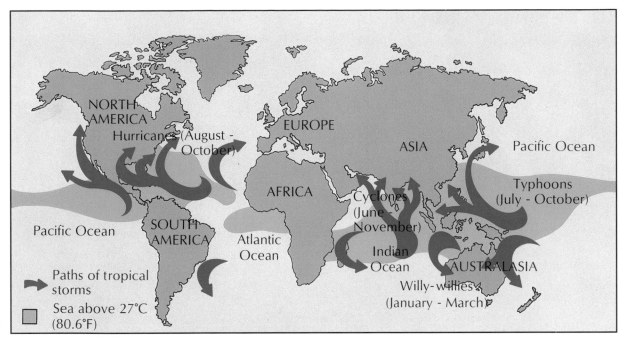

The paths followed by tropical storms. Storms form over warm ocean waters where sea surface temperatures are above 27°C, 80.6°F.

Typhoons, cyclones and a few hurricanes start when southern Trade Winds moving towards the Equatorial Trough push a slight dent in it. A group of thunderstorms in the dent start spinning around. Northern Trade Winds carry off this developing tropical storm. A deepening centre of low pressure, or tropical depression forms in the centre as it spins. Many depressions develop into hurricanes.

A view of a hurricane from space. Winds roar at great speeds around a calm centre.

Weather satellites

The Earth's ever-changing weather may be studied from space using satellites. Orbiting high above its surface, weather satellites take pictures of the Earth day and night using special cameras that detect infra-red or heat radiation.

Some weather satellites circle the Earth at a height of about 900 km, passing over the North and South Poles. On each orbit a strip about 3,500 km wide is photographed around the Earth. As the Earth spins, the satellite is able to photograph the whole surface of the Earth twice every twenty-four hours.

Infra-red cameras detect heat and show different temperatures of land, sea and clouds as different colours. Computers on the ground translate this data into false colour pictures as shown here.

Other weather satellites orbit at a much greater height of 35,800 km. They circle the Earth once every twenty-four hours and can photograph half of the Earth at a time.

Satellites are used for tracking the powerful tropical storms that are common in autumn. They also monitor the advance and retreat of the polar **ice-caps** during autumn and spring and watch the movement of icebergs which are a hazard to shipping.

▲ **As a weather satellite circles the Earth its camera takes a series of overlapping pictures.**

Meteosat II, launched in 1981, orbits 35,800 km above the Equator.

Weather maps and forecasts

Forecasting the weather can be difficult, especially when it is very changeable. Forecasters need to collect information on weather conditions from weather balloons, weather satellites, ships, aircraft and over 5,000 local weather stations all around the world. This information is fed into large computers which make calculations of temperature, air pressure, **humidity**, wind speed and direction. The results are plotted on to maps to help in making the weather forecast.

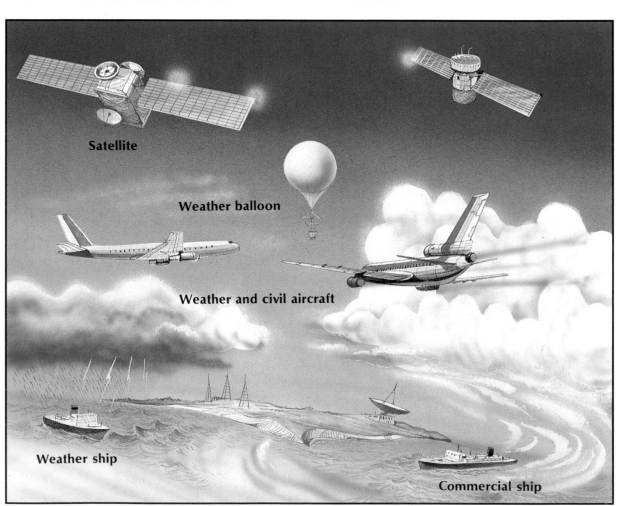

Satellite

Weather balloon

Weather and civil aircraft

Weather ship

Commercial ship

Information about the weather is collected from many sources.

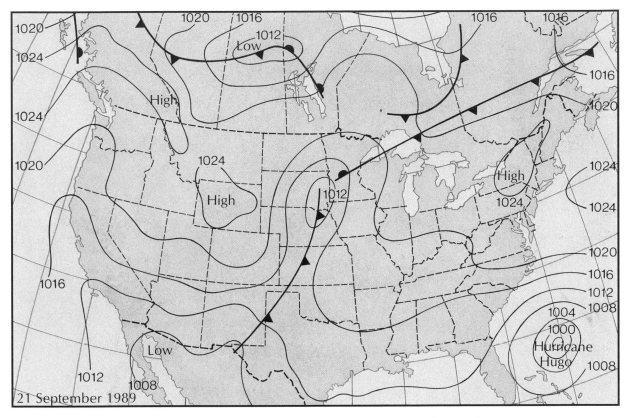

The movement of Hurricane Hugo was closely monitored in autumn 1989.

Weather maps show the roughly circular areas of high and low pressure. The lines which encircle the pressure centres are called isobars, and join places having the same atmospheric pressure. The fronts, where regions of high and low pressure meet, are shown by lines with triangles or semicircles drawn along their length.

Local weather forecasters may look just one or two days ahead. By looking at weather patterns on a world-wide scale, useful weather forecasts for one or two weeks ahead may be produced. The accuracy of these long-range forecasts has been greatly improved by the use of pictures taken from weather satellites.

The Earth's climate

The word climate is used to describe the typical weather conditions at any place over very long periods of time. Today many scientists are asking whether the Earth's climate is getting steadily warmer, or if we are heading for another ice age, when the polar ice-caps will dramatically increase in size.

Trying to predict what will happen is difficult because climatic change is a complex process. Sea temperatures and **ocean currents** cause both long and short-term climatic changes. On several occasions, a rapid warming of the Pacific Ocean by the El Nino current in December has upset the world's weather systems, causing widespread **drought** and **famine** the following autumn.

Changes in the climate also depend on other factors such as the amount of global cloud cover, and the size of the polar ice-caps. The variation in the Sun's heat output and the changes in the Earth's path around the Sun also affect climate. Major volcanic eruptions can cause short-term variations in the climate.

We do not yet know the full long-term effect of the activities of humans on

If further global warming occurs, polar pack ice may melt, causing a rise in sea levels.

climate. Today, most scientists studying the Earth's climate think that it is getting warmer. This is because gases like **carbon dioxide** are released into the air by the burning of coal, gas and oil, and these trap the Sun's heat and cause warming of the atmosphere.

▲ **Factory chimneys belch smoke over Moscow in the USSR.**

The eruption of Mount St. Helens, USA in 1980 caused short-term changes in the Earth's weather patterns.

Drought and famine

Autumn is the season when farmers all over the world gather in their crops and store them for use during the winter. Crops that are sensitive to frosts are harvested before the cold spells arrive. However, particularly early frosts or severe storms can cause devastation, ruining any crops that have not yet been harvested.

Drought is associated with areas of high pressure. The seasonal movement of the world's major high pressure regions is fairly predictable, but sometimes they move further north, sometimes further south than anticipated. Being slow-moving they often stay for too long in one position. If this occurs over several years, the long period of low rainfall may cause severe drought.

In Africa and India, failure of the eagerly awaited rainstorms of the summer **monsoon** can trigger widespread drought.

An Australian sheep farm in autumn after a long drought during the summer months.

A fierce hailstorm has destroyed crops of tea and coffee in Africa.

This causes loss of the year's crops and leads to famine later in the year.

In the Sahel region between the Sahara Desert and rainforests of west Africa, almost no rain fell between 1973 and 1976 because the sub-tropical high pressure area moved further south than usual. This caused widespread famine. Similar weather patterns have occurred in northern Ethiopia, leading to the famine of 1984.

A malnourished child suffering from the effects of a severe famine.

Things to do – measuring wind speed

Autumn can be a very windy season. You can estimate the speed of the wind roughly by using the Beaufort Scale.

The force of the wind can be observed and measured against a scale of 0 (calm) to 12 (hurricane).

	Force	Description	Signs of recognition	Wind speed km/h
			The Beaufort Scale	
	0	Calm	Smoke rises vertically.	0-1
	1	Light air	Smoke drifts slowly in wind.	1-5
	2	Light breeze	Wind felt on face; leaves rustle.	6-11
	3	Gentle breeze	Flags flutter; leaves and twigs move continuously.	12-19
	4	Moderate breeze	Wind raises dust and blows loose paper; small branches move.	20-29
	5	Fresh breeze	Small trees in leaf sway; small wavelets on inland waters.	30-39
	6	Strong breeze	Large branches sway; whistling in telephone wires.	40-50
	7	Near gale	Whole trees sway; inconvenient to walk against wind.	51-61
	8	Gale	Twigs break from trees; difficult to walk; gale warnings on radio.	62-74
	9	Strong gale	Large branches break; slates removed from roofs.	75-87
	10	Storm	Trees uprooted; major damage.	88-101
	11	Violent storm	Usually at sea or in coastal areas; very widespread damage.	102-117
	12	Hurricane	Usually at sea or in coastal areas storm surge; major disaster.	Over 118

An anemometer is the name given to any instrument which measures wind speed. A line of washing blowing in the wind is a very crude anemometer. The faster the wind blows, the more it pushes the clothes on the line towards a horizontal position.

The windsock is a very simple form of anemometer. It consists of a tube of cloth which pivots on top of a pole in the ground. The windsock is blown out at an angle from the pole depending on the wind strength, and indicates both speed and direction.

Taking a wind-speed reading from a hemispherical cup anemometer.

Lines of washing blowing are a simple form of anemometer.

The most widely used instrument for measuring wind speed is the cup anemometer. Three or four hemispherical cups pivot about a vertical spindle and rotate according to the force and speed of the wind pushing upon them. By counting the number of turns of the anemometer in a certain direction, the wind speed can be calculated.

GLOSSARY

Arctic The cold lands and seas around the North Pole.

Carbon dioxide A gas found in air, formed from carbon and oxygen.

Condense To turn water vapour into drops of liquid by cooling.

Dewpoint The temperature at which water vapour in the air starts to condense into water droplets.

Drought A long period of dry weather when no rain falls.

Equator A line that encircles the Earth midway between the North and South Poles.

Evaporate The process by which liquid water becomes a vapour or gas due to heating.

Famine An extreme shortage of food in an area, leading to hunger and starvation.

Front The boundary between a mass of cold and mass of warm air.

Hemisphere Half of the Earth's sphere.

Horizon The line at which the earth and sky appear to meet.

Humidity The amount of moisture in the form of water vapour that there is in the air.

Ice-cap A thick layer of ice lying over a large area of land and completely covering it.

Monsoon A wind that changes direction with the seasons.

Ocean current A moving flow of warmer or cooler water in the ocean.

Poles The extreme north and south of the Earth.

Spectrum The colours produced when white sunlight is dispersed.

Temperate regions The areas having a moderate, mild climate between the tropics and the polar regions.

Trade Winds Strong winds that blow towards the Equator from the north-east in the northern hemisphere and the south-east in the southern hemisphere.

Tropics A band on the Earth's surface stretching between about latitudes 25° north and 25° south of the Equator, where the weather is always warm.

Water vapour Particles of moisture suspended in the air.

Wavelength The distance between the top of one wave and the next in a wave motion.

BOOKS TO READ

Bramwell, Martyn, **Weather** (Franklin Watts, 1987)
Jones, Joan, **Projects for Autumn** (Wayland, 1989)
Pohlman, John, **All about the Weather** (Hamlyn, 1984)
Rosen, Mike, **Autumn Festivals** (Wayland, 1990)
Whitlock, Ralph, **Autumn** (Wayland, 1987)
Whitlock, Ralph, **Weather** (Macdonald Educational, 1985)

PICTURE ACKNOWLEDGEMENTS

The publishers would like to thank the following for allowing their pictures to be reproduced in this book: Bruce Coleman Ltd 13 (bottom); Chris Fairclough Colour Library 9 (top); The Hutchison Library 18, 25 (top), 26; Frank Lane Picture Agency 5 (top), 13 (top), John Mason 19; Oxford Scientific Films 24, 29 (top); Photri cover, 5 (bottom); Science Photo Library 20, 21; Tony Stone Worldwide inside cover, 6, 8, 9 (bottom), 12, 15, 16 (both), 17; Tropix Photo Library 27 (both); Zefa 11, 25 (bottom), 29 (bottom). All illustrations by Hayward Art Group except page 22.

INDEX

Numbers in **bold** refer to illustrations